CISCO CCNA NETWORKING
FOR BEGINNERS

By Adam Vardy

Introduction

I want to thank you and congratulate you for purchasing the book, *"Cisco CCNA Networking for Beginners"*.

Reading this book is only the start of an amazing journey to the world of computer networking as you gear up yourself to pass the Cisco CCNA Routing & Switching 200-120 Exam. This exam is a composite exam and it is a requirement in becoming a Certified Cisco Network Associate.

This book contains the most important topics that frequently appear in the CCNA Exam. The world of computer networking is more complicated than the concepts and principles contained within this book. Many of them are not covered by the CCNA Exam, but still you need to learn and master them if you want to become a reliable network administrator. Consider this book as your study guide that could help you understand the major concepts, primarily when it comes to Cisco Routing & Switching. For detailed examples and more strategies, you must always refer to Cisco official references.

Thanks again for purchasing this book. I hope you enjoy it!

Table Of Contents

Chapter 1 – Networks and their Building Blocks

This chapter will help you understand the fundamental concepts of network: the different types of networks and the devices used in networks. Then, you will learn more about the TCP/IP model and the OSI reference model. These models are crucial to understand not only to pass the CCNA exam, but also to establish underlying concepts that could help your career as a network specialist. In addition, you will also learn about Ethernet Technologies, Network Applications, and Cisco Three Layer Model, which was designed by Cisco to help professionals in designing, implementing, and troubleshooting networks.

Introduction to Networks

A network is a group of interconnected devices such as printers, computers, servers, etc. To understand why networks are crucial, you need to look back to the time when networks were non-existent. Consider a large company that manufactures and sells Ready-to-Wear clothes.

Let's call the company RTW Inc. Just imagine the volume of data needed by the corporate executives to make crucial decisions such as sales, orders, and inventory. Local branch offices had to send collected data through snail mail. It would take three to five days for the main office to receive the data. It will also require people to collect, consolidate, and summarize the data, which increases the chances of human error occurring. This is just one-way data transfer. The local branch offices also need information that is crucial for their operations.

If RWT Inc. exists in the present time, all their offices will be interconnected. They will only use one software program, which will store all the data in one central location. With only a few clicks and within seconds, the executives can have access to real-time data. Because the data is stored in a central hub, any authorized personnel can see the data from any location. It is significantly cheaper to maintain a network because organizations can save time, money, and effort. It directly increases productivity.

Networks also help in maximizing resources through sharing. A basic example of this is printer sharing in an office. Without established networks, every computer will require their own printer. With a network, the printer could be shared between different computers.

Now, let's take a look at how networks work. The most basic form of a network is shown in Figure 1.1. It shows two hosts (devices such as computers) that are directly connected to each other through a network cable. Most end-user devices today are added with Network Interface Card (NIC) for network connection.

HOST A

HOST B

Figure 1.1
Most basic form of network

Host A is connected to the NIC of Host B, which is connected to the network. In this form, the cable is directly connected to another host.

3

Because both hosts are networked, they can share information. This form is effective, but not scalable. If you add another host in this network, it requires another NIC card for every connection, so it is not a practical solution. For three or more hosts, you need a device called hub. Figure 1.2 shows a hub that connects three hosts.

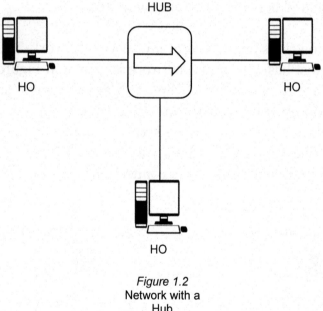

Figure 1.2
Network with a
Hub

A hub can repeat data received from a host to other connections. In Figure 1.2, the hub can repeat any data received from the three hosts, so they are able to communicate with each other.

There are three types of communication between hosts: unicast (one host to another host), broadcast (one host to all hosts), and multicast (one host to selected hosts).

If you use a hub to network hosts, it could result to two types of problems:

1. A hub establishes a shared network where only one host can send data one at a time. If another host tries to send data packets at the same time, it could lead to collision. Each host will then resend the data, hoping that the collision will not happen again. Data collision often results to inefficient network.

2. A hub relays data received from one host to other hosts. For example in Figure 1.2, Host A will send a unicast message to Host B. Once the hub receives this information, it will share the message to Host B and Host C. Although the message was a unicast is intended only for Host B, Host C will also receive the data.

The problems arising from hubs may cause critical degradation to the network. In order to resolve these problems, switches are often used as an alternative to hubs. Similar to hubs, switches are used to network hosts but they prevent collision through a separate collision domain for each port. As the name suggests, switches switch the data from one port to another. But unlike hubs, they don't flood each packet from every port. They switch a unicast packet to the port where the intended host is located. Switches only flood out broadcast packet. Figure 1.3 is an example of a switched network.

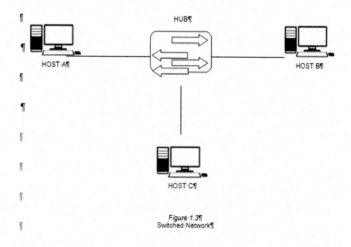

Figure 1.3
Switched Network

Take note that a switch floods out a broadcast packet and not a unicast packet. Every host that is connected to a switched network is virtually located in one broadcast domain. Hence, all the hosts networked to it will receive the message from this domain. Even though broadcasts are crucial for efficient network operations, high volume of broadcasts in a large switched network could slow it down. To resolve this issue, you can break down the networks in smaller sizes, and connect the separate networks through routers. They don't allow broadcasts to be relayed across separate networks but it still connects them allowing more efficient domain. Figure 1.4 shows a router that interconnects three switched networks.

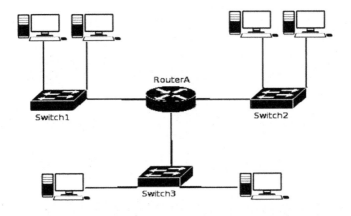

Figure 1.4
Router connecting three
switched networks

In the figure shown above, Switch 2 and Switch 3 will not receive any broadcast from Switch 1 because the router will interfere with the broadcast.

Aside from providing partitions between broadcast domains, routers also have the following important functions:

1. **Network Communication** – As demonstrated in Figure 1.4, routers can allow sharing of information between connected networks.

2. **Packet Switching** – Basically, a router works like a switch, because it can switch packets between networks.

3. **Packet Filtering** – A router can forward or drop packets based on particular factors such as the origin and destination of the packet.

4. **Path Selection** – A router can communicate with other routers to learn essential information about the networks connected to different routers and then choose the best path to relay message to a network.

Always remember that routers break down broadcast domains, while switches break collision domains. Be sure to remember the main functions of the router as it often appears in the CCNA exam.

Types of Networks

Networks are categorized into different types according to their expanse, purpose, security and other factors. It will help your career if you could learn them all, but as regards with the scope of the CCNA exam, you only need to learn two important types of network. As a matter of fact, a significant part of the CCNA exam tackles about these network types:

1. Local Area Network or LAN

This network covers the restricted geographical perimeters such as a building, a floor, or an office. This type of network often has a high rate for data transfer, and the most commonly used technology is the Ethernet standard. Recently, wireless technology is becoming a common technology for local LAN.

2. Wide Area Network or WAN

This network covers a wide geographical location such as a cities, a whole country, a whole continent, or even the whole world. WANs connect the LANs around the area they cover. Different technology standards will be discussed later in this book.

Models of Internetworking

As computers become more essential in our daily lives, companies recognized the need to connect them efficiently and effectively. They designed different protocols with hidden specifications. Therefore, every company had various methods of connecting computer and these methods were not compatible with one another. In the past, the computers of one company cannot be networked with computers produced by another company.

Gradually, the network specifications were publicized and some inter-company compatibility was established. However, there were still some flaws. The International Organization for Standardization (ISO) started to work in 1977 to come up with a public standard networking models that all computers could use. In 1984, the Open Systems Interconnection (OSI) was made public. Simultaneously, the Defense Advanced Research Projects Agency (DAPRA) was also working on a standard network model, which is now known as the TCP/IP Model. This model became more popular compared to the OSI model.

OSI Reference Model

Aside from promoting communication between devices from different vendors, the OSI Reference model also allows communication between separate hosts such as devices using different operating systems (OSX, Windows, or Linux). Take note that a system which still uses OSI protocols is pretty rare so you probably aren't going to work on one. However, it is still crucial to learn this model and the term used because this is often compared to other models especially the TCP/IP model. Therefore, we will only discuss this model from a general perspective.

Similar to other network models, the OSI reference model partitions the protocols, functions, and devices of a network into different layers. This approach provides several benefits, such as:

- Communication is broken down into simpler compositions, which makes planning, creating, and troubleshooting a lot easier

- Alterations in one layer will not affect other layers, so the development in one layer will not be subject to the restrictions of other layers
- It permits different types of software and hardware to easily communicate with each other
- Simple mechanism to standardize functions because they are divided into smaller parts
- Because of its layered structure, the vendors can write to a common output and input specification for each layer

The Seven Layers of OSI Reference Models

Figure 1.5 shows the seven layers of the OSI Reference Model and a summarized version of their primary functions.

7. APPLICATION	Provides a user interface
6. PRESENTATION	Manages encryption and decryption and presents data
5. SESSION	Provides dialog control between hosts and keeps the distinction between data of independent applications
4. TRANSPORT	Provides delivery and flow control and provides end-to-end connections
3. NETWORK	Provides Path determination through logical addressing
2. DATA LINK	Provides physical addressing and media access
1. PHYSICAL	Digital data conversion and data movement between hosts

Figure 1.5
Seven Layers of OSI
Reference Model

It is crucial to take note of the names of the OSI layers including their functions. One good way to remember them is to use this mnemonic: **A**ll **P**eople **S**eem **T**o **N**eed **D**ata **P**rocessing. This might appear in your CCNA exam.

TCP/IP Model

Similar to the OSI reference model, the TCP/IP model also follows a layered structure, but already a shortened version with its four layers: application, transport, internet, and network access. The functions of these layers are similar to the functions of the seven layers composing the OSI model. Below is a detailed discussion of the four layers of the TCP/IP model, including their protocols.

Application Layer is composed of different protocols, which perform all the functions of three layers in the OSI Reference Model: Application, Presentation, and Session. It also includes the interaction with the application, data encoding and translation, coordination of communication and control of dialogue throughout the systems.

Examples of Application layer protocols used today are Telnet, HTTP, FTP, SMTP, TFTP, DNS, and DHCP.

Transport Layer

All application layer protocols take user data and integrate a header and relay it to the Transport layer that will be sent across the network. The

Transport Layer of the TCP/IP model is similar to the Transport Layer of the OSI Model. It covers the end-to-end transportation of data and establishes an efficient connection between the hosts.

There are two available protocols in the Transport Layer: the User Datagram Protocol (UDP) and the Transmission Control Protocol (TCO). Basically, UDP relays the data without the frills, while the TCP is a connection-oriented protocol that utilizes the windowing approach to regulate the flow and provide more organized delivery of segmented data. Even though these two protocols have numerous differences, they perform similar function of relaying data through the use of port numbers.

Most application layer protocols are assigned with port numbers from 1 to 1024. Applications that are using these protocols "listen" to these numbers. UDP and TCO on the destination host know which application to send the data in reference with the port numbers assigned. Table 1.1 shows the most common port numbers.

Application Protocol	Transport Protocol	Port Number
DNS	TCP, UDP	53
FTP (Control)	TCP	21
FTP (Data)	TCP	20
HTTP	TCP	80
HTTPS	TCP	443
SMTP	TCP	25
SSH	TCP	22
Telnet	TCP	23
TFTP	UDP	69

It is crucial to remember the application layer protocols listed above and their assigned port numbers as they often appear in the CCNA exam, usually in an access-list item or in a multiple choice question.

The Internet Layer

The Internet Layer of the TCP/IP model is parallel to the Network Layer of the OSI reference model in terms of function. It covers path determination, path forwarding, and logical addressing.

The well-known protocol that provides these services is the Internet Protocol or IP. Also included in this layer are routing protocols that support the routers in learning about the various networks that they communicate and the Internet Control Message Protocol (ICMP) for communicating error messages. CCNA syllabus mostly covers the IP and Routing protocols so you can learn more about them in the succeeding chapters.

Network Access Layer

The TCP/IP Model's Network Access Layer is parallel with the Data Link Layer and Physical Layer of the OSI model. This layer outlines the hardware and protocols needed to establish connection between a host and a physical network in order to effectively and efficiently deliver data. The data packets from the Internet Layer are relayed to the Network Access Layer to be delivered to the physical network. The end point could be a host within a network or a router that will forward the data.

The Network Access Layer is composed of wide range of protocols. If the physical network is the LAN, the commonly used protocol is the Ethernet. However, if the physical network is a WAN, the commonly used protocols could be Frame Relay and Point-to-Point Protocol (PPP).

Bear in mind that Network Access Layer uses a physical address to define hosts and deliver data. Its PDU called a frame, which contains the IP packet and a protocol header and trailer from the layer.

Ethernet Technologies and Cabling

Ethernet refers to the family of standards defining the Network Access Layer of most types of LAN today. The different standards may vary in terms of cable types, speeds supported, and cable lengths. The organization that is in charge of defining the different standards is the Institute of Electrical and Electronics Engineers (IEEE).

The IEEE divides the functions of the Data Link into two sublayers: Logical Link Control (LLC) 802.2 and the Media Access Control (MAC) 802.3 sublayer.

Ethernet uses the contention media access approach to permit all hosts within a network for sharing the bandwidth. Several hosts are trying to utilize the media in transferring data. Once multiple hosts simultaneously send traffic, a collision may occur that could lead to data loss. Take note that the Ethernet cannot prevent that completely; however, it can detect such a collision and perform corrective actions through the Carrier Sense Multiple Access with Collision Detection (CSMA/CD) protocol.

Physical Layer of the Ethernet

The group of companies composed of Digital, Xerox, and Intel originally developed and used the Ethernet. In 1982, IEEE took over and developed the 802.3 standard or the 10Mbps, which used co-axial cables. Eventually, IEEE extended the 802.3 sublayer into two: FastEthernet (802.3u) and the Gigabit Ethernet (802.3ab). Then it developed the 10Gbps over fiber and co-axial (802.3ae).

Meanwhile, the Electronics Industries Association and the newer Telecommunication Industries Alliance (EIA/TIA) is the organization that develops the physical layer specs for the Ethernet. It established the Registered Jack (RJ) connector with the 4 5 wiring sequence on an unshielded twisted-pair (UTP) cabling as a standard.

There are three types of cables used in connecting different types of devices: normal patch cable (straight cable), crossover cable, and rolled cable.

Normal Patch Cables

A UTP cable contains eight wires. A normal patch cable uses four out of these eight wires. Figure 1.6 demonstrates the wire configurations for normal patch cable. Take note that only the wires 1,2,3, and 6 are connected to the matching number on the other end.

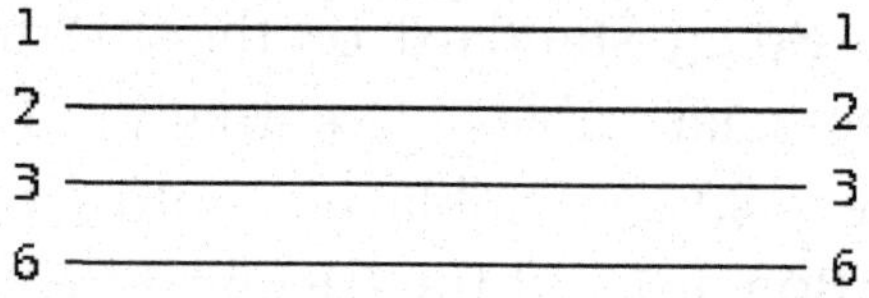

Figure 1.6
Wire Configurations of
Normal Patch Cable

Crossover Cables

Crossover cable also utilizes the same four wires used in a normal patch cable, but they are connected to different pins as shown in Figure 1.7.

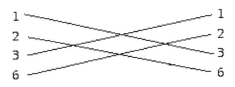

Figure 1.7
Wire Configurations of
Crossover Cable

Crossover cables are used to connect host to host, hub to hub, switch to switch, switch to hub, and router to a host. The best way to remember this is that same devices are linked to each other through crossover cables.

Rolled Cables

You can't use rolled cables for Ethernet connection, because these are used for connecting to the console ports of routers or switches from the serial communication port of the host. Take note that Cisco routers and switches are added with console ports used for configurations. All eight wires are connected in the cable and every wire is connected to the opposite number as shown in Figure 1.8.

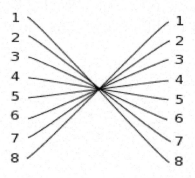

Figure 1.8
Wire Configurations of
Rolled Cables

The types of cables and their uses are crucial topics that you must master not only to pass the CCNA Exam but also to become a successful network specialist.

The Three-Layer Model of Cisco

In large organizations, it's common to see complex networks composed of many devices, locations, protocols, and services. This can be difficult to manage and troubleshoot these complicated networks. Networks must ride on with the technological developments, so making changes to a complicated network is usually problematic.

With its vast experience in network equipment and managing its own network, Cisco has developed a three-layer model. This structure offers a modular approach of establishing networks, which makes it easy for implementation, management, scaling, and troubleshooting of networks.

The three-layer model of Cisco is composed of the Core layer, the Distribution layer, and the Access layer. These are logical layers, and each has its own particular functions.

The **Core Layer** is the foundation of the internetwork. It is the most basic but the most important layer with its primary function of transporting huge amount of data within a specific time frame. It sources out the data from the Distribution layer and sends it back after transportation.

The **Distribution Layer** serves as the interface between the Core and the Access layers. The main function of this layer is the provision of filtering, routing, and access to WAN and to determine how packets could access the core, if necessary. Determining the path is the most crucial function of this layer. It should choose the quickest way that an access request could be fulfilled. It also serves as the convergence point for all switches of the access layer.

The **Access Layer** is the point in the network where different devices such as Desktop computers, laptops, printers, and other gadgets are connected to the network. The regular resourced required by users are available at this layer while request access to remote resources are relayed to the distribution layer.

Chapter 2 – IP Addressing and Subnets

In the first chapter, you have learned the different layers of the TCP/IP model. Bear in mind that the CCNA Exams is virtually about the Internet and Network Access Layer. In this chapter, you will learn about IP Addresses, which is one of the most significant areas in networking.

Remember, every host in the network is assigned with a logical address, which is known as the IP address. Indicating address to a network assists in routing packets from origin to endpoint all throughout in the networks.

The length of an IP address is 32 bits. In order for the address to be easier to read, it is partitioned into four sections with eight bits separated by a period. Hence, every section is one byte. To make it even easier to read, the binary numbers are transformed to decimals. For instance, an IP address like 01111100011010101010111100110101 is separated into eight bits leading to: 01111100.01101010.10101111.00110101. When you transform this into decimal, it will become 124.106.175.53, which is called the dotted decimal format. There are available online applications, which convert the address to hexadecimal format rather than the decimal format. But this is rare to appear in the CCNA exam, so you need to focus in mastering the dotted decimal format.

Aside from the host address, the IP address also signifies the network where the host is located as well as the host itself. As such, the IP address is composed of two parts: the Network component, which defines the network within an internetwork and the Host component, which defines the host itself in the network. Every mixture of the host component and the network component must be unique for the whole Internetwork. For easier identification of these two parts, addresses are categorized into five classes.

Class A is for an internetwork with limited number of networks and wide range of hosts for every network. The first eight bits are known as the network component, while the rest of the 24 bits are the host component.

Class B serves as the bridge between Class A and Class C, because it provides average number of networks with average number of hosts. The first 16 bits refer to the network component while the three bytes are the host components.

Class C provides for a large number of networks with limited number of hosts for every network. The first 24 bits refer to the network component while the last eight bits refer to the host components.

Class D is used for multi-casting, while Class E comprises reserved addresses.

Take note that if every host bits in a particular address are set to zero (0), then it is signified as a network address. Meanwhile, if every host bits are set to one (1), then it signified broadcast address. Remember, these addresses must not be assigned to a host.

Subnetting

Class A and Class B addresses can provide for a large number of hosts. Class A has a total of 16,777,216 hosts, while Class B has a total of 65,534 hosts. As you have already learned in the first chapter, there are some disadvantages when it comes to large networks, so it will help a lot if they are divided into smaller networks connected via routers. Setting up a network with the total number of hosts permitted for both classes will only lead to problems. On the other hand, setting up small networks with these classes will waste the rest of the addresses.

In order to resolve this problem, you can establish connections through subnetting. This method allows you to derive some host bits and use them in creating more networks. These are known as subnets and are smaller in size. But because every network has a broadcast address and a network address, there are addresses that will go to waste.

To understand more the benefit of subnetting, consider a Class C address. Every class C address allows 254 hosts. If you need two networks with 100 addresses, and you use two class C networks, the remaining 308 addresses will go to waste. Rather than using two Class C networks, you can try subnetting one obtain two networks that will allow 126 addresses. With this, you can lessen the number of idle addresses.

There are also problems that arise with subnetting. In the case of class-based subnetting, the first octet of the address in the dotted decimal address signifies which component of the address is the network component and which is the host component. But if the bits are derived for subnetting, the class based restrictions are not applicable, and it could be difficult to identify the network bits. In order to resolve this, subnet masks should be added.

Similar to IP addresses, the length of the subnet mask is 32 bits. The subnet mask value signifies which bits of the address are host component and which are for networks. In a subnet mask, if the value is 1, it signifies that the corresponding bit in the IP address is a network component. The value of 0, on the other hand, signifies that the bit is a host component. Subnet masks are either represented in two forms: Dotted Decimal and Classless Inter-Domain Routing (CIDR) notation.

It is very crucial to understand subnet masks in the Dotted Decimal form or in the CIDR form. Also remember that there is one restriction in subnet masks. All network bits and host bits must be contiguous. Hence, something that appears as 11100100.11110100.11110000.11110000 is not a subnet mask because the network and host bits are not contiguous or adjoining.

Variable Length Subnet Masks (VLSM)

The classless networking approach was introduced through the Variable Length Subnet Masks (VLSM) primarily to avoid the use of various subnet masks across the network for the same class of addresses. For instance, a /30 subnet mask that provides two host addresses for every subnet could be used for point-to-point links in between the routers.

There are two main restrictions that you need to consider if you want to use VLSM: 1.) You need to use fixed block sizes, and 2) You need to use routing protocols, which support classless routing such as Open Shortest Path First (OSPF) Interior Gateway Routing Protocol (EIGRP), Routing Information Protocol (RIP) V2, or Border Gateway Protocol (BGP). Take note that classful protocols, like the RIP Version 1, are not compatible with VLSM.

If you want to use VLSM in designing a network, you must follow these steps in order to come up with the right addressing scheme:

1. Find the largest subnet in the network. Take note that the number of host addresses required decides the size of the subnet.

2. Assign a proper mark to the largest subnet through the fixed block sizes

3. Take note of the subnet numbers remaining in the mask you have used in the second step.

4. Get the remaining subnet and subnet it to provide more space for your smaller subnets

5. Take note of the new subnet numbers again

6. Repeat the fourth and the fifth step for smaller segments

Route Summarization

In the previous chapter, you already know that routers work by setting up a table of all the networks they communicate with. This table is known as the routing table, and the routers use routing protocols to communicate with each other. As the network expands, the routing table also expands its number of entries. Bigger routing tables may lead to increased processing as well as delayed response time. In order to lessen the table sizes, you can group the networks together or summarize them through a mask that can integrate them all.

Route summarization follows the same concept behind VLSM, but in the opposing direction. In using VLSM, you progress to the right, while in summarization, you are progressing to the left. Take note that you can only summarize in block sizes of 128, 64, 32, 16, 8, and 4. Meanwhile, the network address used for the summarized address signifies the first network address contained in the block.

Common Utilities to Troubleshoot IP Addresses

By now, you already know that IP addresses are crucial part of networking and considering the complex nature of addressing and subnetting, it is natural that there will be errors in the network. Hence, it is important for you to troubleshoot common problems that are related to IP Addressing. Before you troubleshoot a network, you must first understand the common protocols and tools used in troubleshooting IP addresses.

Packet Internet Grouper (PING)

This is a very common utility in troubleshooting IP addressing and problems with internet connection. This utility comes free with most operating systems and could be accessed through the command prompt interface through the **ping** command. It checks whether the host is live or not through the use of ICMP protocol.

ARP Table

In some cases, it is a good idea to look at the ARP Table of a network, which contains the MAC address to IP address bindings obtained by the network. The ARP Table could be accesses by using the **arp-a** command. But on a Cisco device, it can be accesses through the show **ip arp** command.

Traceroute

This is another common utility that comes with most operating systems. In some OS, the utility could be viewed by using the **traceroute** command or **tracert** on the CLI. This is used to find every hop between the source and destination hosts and useful to check the path taken by the packet.

IP Config

There are instances that you need to verify the IP address, default gateway, DNS addresses and subnet mask that the host is using. If you are using Windows, you can access this by using the **ipconfig/all** command, and if you are using a Unix based system, this utility can be accessed by using the **ifconfig** command.

Chapter 3 – Cisco Switches, Routers, and IOS

In the first two chapters, you have learned the fundamentals of networking. By now you have the basic knowledge on the different layers of the OSI and TCP/IP models as well as the devices that work on them, specifically switches and routers.

Before learning the different functions in detail, it is important to know what makes them run. This chapter covers the Cisco Internetwork Operating System or IOS, which is a proprietary operating system enabling the Cisco routers and switches on. In this chapter, you will learn about connectivity options, boot process, and methods to configure the devices and access basic verification and config commands.

Cisco Integrated Services Router (ISR)

Cisco supplies different models and series of routers that are designed for various types of users and their requirements. Some of the devices are just for routing while others also provide Wireless connectivity, Voice-over-IP (VoIP) services, and Security features. A great example of routers that offer different services are the routers under the Cisco ISR series.

The focus of the previous CCNA exams were on the 2600 and 2500 routers, which are already retired and now replaced by the 2800/2900 and ISR 1800 routers. Today, the 2600 and 2500 routers are not for sale anymore. Figure 3.1 shows the front panel of the Cisco 1841 router, while Figure 3.2 shows the rear panel of the router with important parts labeled.

Figure 3.1
Front View of Cisco 1841
Router

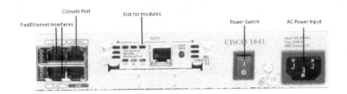

Figure 3.2
Rear View of Cisco 1841
Router

The **FastEthernet interfaces** are used to connect the network to the router. Various routers have different number of interfaces, and many of them are added with slots that you can use to connect a module for more interfaces. In addition to FastEthernet interfaces, a router could also have an ADSL interface, serial interfaces for WAN, and other interfaces.

The **Console Port** is used to establish a connection to the router in order to monitor, configure, or troubleshoot the network.

Some routers are added with **additional slots for modules**, which often add interfaces to the router.

Of course, the **power switch** turns on or off the router, while the **AC Power Input** provides the power supply.

Take note that the CCNA Exam is not fixated on specific devices only. You can still practice using a 2600 or 2500 router, but it is ideal if you could practice using the latest routers. Each command described in this study guide are still applicable in these routers. The only difference that you must be aware of is the output difference in interface type, number of interfaces, and memory.

Cisco IOS

The Cisco Internetwork Operating System (IOS) is a proprietary kernel developed by the company to control all functions of their routers and switches. This is based on the OS system developed by William Yeager in 1980s. This OS allocates resources and oversees actions such as security and hardware interfaces.

The following essential items are covered by the Cisco IOS:

- Connection of high speed traffic between different devices
- Implementation of network functions and protocols
- Controlling access and stopping unauthorized network use by adding security
- Ensuring scalability for effective network growth
- Ensuring reliability of the network to establish the connection to network resources

The Cisco IOS also enables the Command Line Interface or CLI for management, configuration, troubleshooting, and monitoring. The CLI can be viewed through the console port, Telnet, SSH or auxiliary port if available. Take note that the Telnet and SSH both requires IP connectivity, so you need to access the device through the console port.

How to Connect to the CLI through the Console Port

In order to access the CLI of the Cisco switch or router, you need to establish a connection between the PC and the console port of the device. In a Cisco switch or router, the console port is often in form of the RJ45 port. Hence, you need to use a UTP rollover cable with this port and connect it into the console port. There will be a nine-pin serial connection on one end. Plug this into the nine-pin serial port of your device. A blue console cable is always included when you buy a Cisco device. But most computers today don't come with a nine-pin serial port so you may need to buy the serial cable as well as a USB converter.

Connect the serial port of your computer to the serial connection and the RJ45 connector to the router's console port. Once you connect everything to their proper ports, you need to use the Terminal Emulator software to easily access the CLI. Computers running on Windows are included with the HyperTerminal, which is an example of a Terminal Emulator. If your computer runs on Unix, you can use the Minicom, which is a free to download emulator.

Configuring Router Interfaces

Configuring router interfaces is among the basic things that you must learn first before moving on. Take note that the router should be properly connected to the network before it can do its role. The configuration process is normally easy and would only take two steps. But before that, you should first learn about their numbering.

You can see the type and number of interfaces when you boot up your computer. Although there are many varied types of interfaces, which could be present in a router, there are three primary types that frequently appear in the CCNA exam. These are FastEthernet, Ethernet, and Serial. Several of these interfaces are already added into the device, while some are added as modules in available slots. The modules are added into the slot numbers beginning from 1, while the built-in devices go into the slot zero.

Learning the right numbering for interfaces is crucial because you need to know which interface to configure. Take a look at a set-up where the Ethernet cable is connected into the second interface of the second module, while you are setting up the first interface in the first module. The question mark on the CLI could help in determining the format of the numbering in using the interface command in the global config mode. In the output below, you can see the different types of interfaces that can be configured.

```
myRouter(config)#interface ?
Async           Async interface
BVI             Bridge-Group Virtual Interface
CDMA-Ix         CDMA Ix interface
CTunnel         CTunnel interface
Dialer          Dialer interface
FastEthernet    FastEthernet IEEE 802.3
Group-Async     Async Group interface
Lex             Lex interface
Loopback        Loopback interface
MFR             Multilink Frame Relay bundle interface
Multilink       Multilink-group interface
Null            Null interface
Tunnel          Tunnel interface
Vif             PGM Multicast Host interface
```

In the output below, the only available single slot number is zero.

```
myRouter(config)#interface FastEthernet ?
<0-0>  FastEthernet interface number
```

In the output below, you will notice that there are two FastEthernet Interfaces, which can be configured to 1 or 0.

```
myRouter(config)#interface FastEthernet 0?
/

myRouter(config)#interface FastEthernet 0/?
<0-1> FastEthernet interface number
```

In the final output below, take note that the main built-in interface was chosen. Once the prompt changes to config-if, it will be easy to configure different parameters such as speed, protocols, IP address, and duplex for Serial Interfaces.

```
myRouter(config)#interface FastEthernet 0/0 ?
<cr>

myRouter(config)#interface FastEthernet 0/0
myRouter(config-if)#
```

Configuring DNS

In working with advanced configurations such as access lists and routing on IOS devices, you also need to refer to other devices. You can do this by either using hostnames or IP address. Taking note and using IP address of different devices is near impossible and difficult to troubleshoot. Thus, IOS offers two methods to identify names of IP address.

The most common method is to access a DNS server, which you may already have in your network. Just add the IP address of the DNS service by using the ip-name-server command. You can include as many DNS servers as you want. The IOS will communicate to these servers in a series until it receives a reply. When you have included a DNS server, each time the device discovers a name, it will resolve it through server query.

Another method is creating a name map to IP addresses within the IOS. These mappings are also known as host tables. Take note that this method doesn't convert the IOS as a DNS server. It simply set ups a local list for the router. In order to do this, you can use the ip host **name ip_address** command.

Backing Up Configuration

Remember, changes in the configuration are made through the running-config that is distinct from the start-up confic viewed during the boot up. If you fail to save the running-config to the NVRAM as start-up config, the changes will be erased during the reboot.

In order to save the running-config, you need to enter the exec mode and use the copy command. You need to supply two important parameters: the source (running-config) and the destination (startup-config). Hence, the command that you must use is copy running-config startup-config as you will see below.

```
myRouter#copy running-config startup-config
Destination filename [startup-config]?
Building configuration...
[OK]
```

Let's assume that you have made changes in the running-config, but you want to erase them. Take note that changes made in this parameter are implemented instantly. Hence, you can discard all the changes you have made one by one or just copy the startup config to the running config through the copy command. You can just reverse the source and destination.

```
myRouter#copy startup-config running-config
Destination filename [running-config]?
```

Aside from copying the config between startup and running, you can also backup by copying the config between startup and running. It is important to back up the config so that you will have a copy that you can use if the router crashes and you need a replacement.

If you need to clear up the configuration to start again, you can erase the start-up config and reload the router. You can use the command: startup-config while in the exec mode as you will see below:

```
myRouter#erase startup-config
Erasing the nvram filesystem will remove all configuration files! Continue? [confirm]
[OK]
Erase of nvram: complete
```

How to Recover Password on a Cisco Router

It is common for users to forget passwords when working with IOS based devices. While the process of recovering password differ from devices, most routers have similar process for password recovery.

Password recovery for Cisco switches is quite different and not included in the CCNA exam, so we'll just look at the password recovery for Cisco routers.

First, you need to understand two important things linked with the boot process:

Configuration Register

This is a 16-bit value, written to the NVRAM and control parameters of the boot process. You can change this once the bootstrap program explores the IOS file, if the startup config is loaded and even if the boot process must stop at ROMmon and the IOS file should not be loaded.

There are two values that you should take note during the configuration register: 2142 and 2102. The value 2142 signifies that the router will not load the startup config but will load the IOS file from the flash. The config register's value could be viewed in the output using the **show version** command.

ROM Monitor

This is also known as the bootstrap program, which locates and boots the IOS file, and initializes the hardware. This mode could be used for testing and troubleshooting. If the IOS file cannot be loaded during the boot up, you will be transformed into the ROM monitor mode. The prompt for this is rommon#>, where # signifies a number. There are few commans that you can use in this mode to find and troubleshoot problems connected with the boot up. This can also be used to copy IOS files to the flash from TFTP.

The ROM Monitor and the Configuration Register are crucial to recover password. The primary steps are the following:

1. Start the device through the ROM Monitor mode

2. Adjust the Configuration Register so that the startup config will not be loaded

3. Start into the IOS

4. Access the exec mode and copy the startup config into the running config

5. Enter new passwords

6. Save the running config into the startup config

7. Modify the config register to 2102

8. Restart the device

So basically, you need to make sure that the router loads the IOS devoid of the startup config. With this, you can work on exec mode even without a password. Then, you can load the startup config and enter new password and save back the configuration.

In order to boot into the ROM Monitor mode, you need to reboot the device and break the sequence of the boot. You can do this by pressing Ctrl + Break key while the system is booting. However, the break sequence may vary depending on the client and the operating system. For instance, if you are using OSX, you need to use the Cmd + b. But for the CCNA Exam, the Ctrl + Break is the only choice. You can practice more on this by using the Windows/Hyperterminal application.

Chapter 4 – Understanding IP Routing

IP Routing refers to the process of moving packets from a source to a destination throughout the networks. In order to successfully route packets, a router should know the following data: address of the destination, potential routes to all remote networks, nearby routers from which it could discover remote networks, and the best route for every remote network. The router should be able to preserve and verify these routing data.

Routing data is stored in the Routing Information Base (RIB), which is also known as the routing table. Every route is an integration of the destination network address, the next move towards the destination, and the subnet mask. There are three main ways for a router to understand routes:

1. Default Routing

In Default Routing, all routers are configured to send all the packets towards one router. This is a useful approach for simple networks or for networks with only one exit and entry point.

2. Static Routing

In Static Routing, you can manually add routes to the RIB. This is often used for small networks and not recommended for large networks.

3. Dynamic Routing

In Dynamic Routing, the algorithms and protocols are used to immediately broadcast routing data. This is a complex yet common routing method.

Three Classes of Routing Protocols

Routing protocols are categorized into three classes, based on their functions.

1. Link State Protocols

Link State Protocols form a remote connection with other routers prior to sharing routing data. They don't broadcast routing data to the whole network. Routing data are all stores in a table. These protocols only share connectivity data or link states, which are stored in a topology table to establish a general prospect of the network. In reference to the links received, every router computes the best path for each network destination. Every protocol has its own algorithm to figure out the best path.

Distance Vector Protocols

Distance Vector Protocols use distance to measure the route cost. The number of hops between the router and a destination network establishes the distance. They regularly send their whole routing table to the remote routers. The receiving router then integrates its routing table with the received data based on the metrics. This process is also known as rumor routing, because the end router will believe the information received from its neighbor.

In comparison with Link State Protocols, Distance Vector Protocols take more time to converge. A network can only be considered fully converged if all the network routers learn all destination networks. However, they are easier to manage, configure, and troubleshoot. On the other hand, they require more bandwidth and memory because they regularly send the whole routing table, even if there are no changes. A good example of a Distance Vector Protocol is RIP.

3. Hybrid Protocols

Hybrid Protocols use features of both Link State Protocols and Distance Vector Protocols. A good example of a hybrid protocol is the EIGRP.

Take note that the distinctions between the different protocol classes as well as the examples for every class are a recurring topic in the CCNA Exam.

Routing Loops

A routing loop is a condition wherein a packet is routed between several routers because of some issues in the routing table. This is often the case with Distance Vector Protocols when they are rumor routing and have slow convergence could result to routing loops. To learn more about how routing loops can happen with Distance Vector Protocols, take a closer look at Figure 4.1 below:

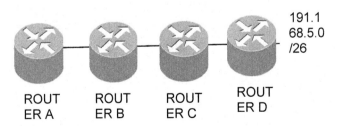

191.1
68.5.0
/26

ROUT
ER A

ROUT
ER B

ROUT
ER C

ROUT
ER D

Figure 4.1
Routing Loops

Once converged, the router networks above will discover the 191.168.5.0.0/26 network. When Router D loses connection to 191.168.5.0.0/26, it will erase the route to that network from its table. If Router C gets the next regular update from Router D, it will discover that the route to 191.168.5.0.0/26 has been lost, and thus will be erased from the routing table. At this point, Router A and Router B will still believe that the 191.168.5.0.0/26 network is reachable through the Router C.

At the time Router C stands idle to wait for the update, when Router B deploys its own update, it will contain the 191.168.5.0.0/26 network as its destination. Because Router C doesn't have that network in its routing table, it will believe that it's a fresh destination and Router B believes about and will still install the route to that network, directed towards Router B. From this, the regular update from Router C will still contain the 191.168.5.0.0/26 network and Router B will believe that it is aware of all the networks contained in the update.

Once Router B receives a packet intended for 191.168.5.0.0/26, it will send it to the Router C. Once Router C receives this packet it will make sure that the 191.168.5.0.0/26 is directed towards Router B and will send it back. This loop shall continue until the IP TTL value in the packet reaches zero and a router drops it.

In order to avoid routing loops, Distance Vector Protocols have established some restraints, as discussed below.

Split Horizon

The split horizon control ensures that the routing data learned from an interface cannot be sent back to that interface. With this control measure added in the above network, Router B will never send 191.168.5.0.0/26 network back to Router C, because that's the origin of the route. So, a routing loop will never take in the first place. As a default feature, the Split Horizon is added for EIGRP and RIP.

Hold Down Timers

Routing protocols add timers to recover lost routers or to change to the next best route to the same destination. These are known as hold-down timers, which is ideal to use if links are going up and down rapidly. This could cause loops and stop the network from convergence. Hold downs also avoid changes that affect a route that was just lost.

In the example above, hold down timers could block the Router B update from affecting the Router C after the route to 191.168.5.0.0/26 was lost. Meanwhile, Router C would send update to Router B about the lost route.

Maximum Hop Count

Without controls in place, the incorrect routing data could spread all throughout the network. In order to prevent this, the protocols such as RIP have maximum hop count. The maximum hop count for RIP is 15. A route with higher maximum hop count will be unreachable and cannot be used.

In the above network, the primary hop count of 191.168.5.0.0/26 on Router B was only 2. When Router A lost its connection, and Router C received the wrong data, it would see 191.168.5.0.0/26 with 3 hop counts. Once Router B gets this update from Router C, it will add another hop count and will make it 4. This cycle will continue. Without an established maximum hop count, this will proceed. This is known is known as counting to infinity. Without the established maximum hop count, the accumulation of added hop counts will cause the routes to be unreachable, and will be eliminated from the routing table that will cause the loop to be resolved.

Route Poisoning

Route poisoning prevent network loops through the use of maximum hop counts. Once a router looses a route, it sends message that route with a hop count reaching beyond the maximum hop count. The destination router will find the destination network unreachable and will broadcast it ahead. This will also send update towards the source router to make certain that the router is now poisoned in the whole network. This process is known as poison reverse.

In the example above, if Router D lost 191.168.5.0.0/26, it will relay the route to Router C with a hop count beyond the maximum hop count. In turn, Router C will update Router B. This is the process of route poisoning. Router C will also send the poisoned route back to Router D to make certain that the entire network is synchronized. This is called the poison reverse process.

All the methods used in preventing routing loops are essential topics and would probably be covered in the CCNA Exam.

Chapter 5 – Network Security

Cisco routers running on Cisco IOS are added with security tools, which can be used as part of a sound security strategy. Access Control Lists (ACL) is regarded as the most important security tool in Cisco IOS software. They can be used to outline controls to avoid some packets from flowing through the network.

Cisco also manufactures a range of specialized security devices such as the Adaptive Security Appliance (ASA), which companies can use for securing their networks.

Confidentiality, Integrity, and Availability (CIA) Model

A security structure is a structure, which provides guiding principles to secure the systems to meet industry regulations and best practices. A broadly applicable model of network security is the Confidentiality, Integrity, and Availability (CIA), which serve as the guiding principles that can be used to secure the systems. Violation of these principles could lead to large security consequences.

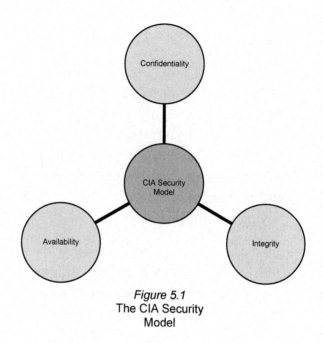

Figure 5.1
The CIA Security
Model

Confidentiality

Confidentiality refers to the prevention of sensitive data from being viewed by unauthorized people. It is the capacity to make certain that the minimum level of security is implemented and data is concealed from unauthorized people. Information is a highly valuable asset, and securing sensitive data is important for organizations. This is the reason why Confidentiality is the security aspect that comes under attack by those who want to discover crucial information for their own interests. Data encryption is the primary method to protect data confidentiality of information transferred from device to another.

Integrity

Integrity refers to the prevention of any unauthorized changes of data to ensure accuracy. With integrity, the user can be certain that it is the real unmodified information and so it can be a reliable piece of information. A common type of attack that affects data integrity is known as the middle-man attack, in which the attacker interrupts the information while in transit and make modifications to it that are unknown to the two communicating parties.

Availability

Availability refers to the prevention of data and resources loss and making certain that they are ready for use if they are needed. It is crucial to ensure that information is always available at all times so that authorized requests could be provided. Denial of Service (DoS) is a common type of security attack that tries to interrupt the immediate access to data and resource, which compromises the availability of systems.

Cisco Firewalls

Firewalls are essential component of a network security framework, and Cisco provides firewall solutions in varying types. The common Cisco firewalls are Cisco IOS Firewalls, Cisco PIX 500 Series of Firewalls, Cisco ASA 5500 series Adaptive Security Appliances, and Cisco Firewall Services Module.

Layer 2 Security

Always bear in mind that a network security is only as formidable as the weakest link. A seemingly small weak spot if penetrated successfully would be sufficient for an attacker to access the whole network. The weak spot could be the Data Link Layer or the Second Layer of the OSI reference model. You can secure the posterior of the network to safeguard it against threats, but it is also crucial to secure the network interior as some threats could even come from the interior.

Similar to routers, Cisco switches also have their integral set of network security requirements. In fact, switches could turn out to be that weak spot if not secured appropriately. Gaining access to switches could be an easy entry point for intruders who want to penetrate the network.

When an intruder gains access to a switch, it is easy to launch any form of attack from inside the network. The security measures that are designed to protect the network will not be sufficient to avert these attacks because they are coming from inside the network.

Cisco Port Security

One way to enhance the security of the switches and the whole network is by adding port security on Cisco switches to control who can access the network by connecting to a switch port. The switch port can be configured and can also figure out the addresses that are allowed to access the port. The secure switch port does not forward frames with source addresses outside the group of specified addresses for a particular port.

AAA Security Services

Authentication, Authorization, and Accounting (AAA) Security Services refers to a framework, which you can use to create access control on Cisco switches, routers, firewalls and other network devices. This security framework provides you the ability to specify who is permitted to access network devices, and what services the user must be allowed for access.

This framework is often used to control console access to network devices or telnet.

AAA uses TACACS+, Kerberos, and RADIUS as authentication protocols to supervise its security functions. A Cisco router requiring AAA services will set up a connection to the security server by using any of these protocols. The security server is a Linux or Windows host that is external to the network device, and includes a database that contains the user names and passwords. Within a Cisco network device, AAA can also be configured to use a local registry of user names and passwords. You need to use the global configuration command: aaa new-model to enable the AAA.

Chapter 6 – Wide Area Networks

By using a Wide Area Network (WAN), you can extend the Local Area Network (LAN) to nearby LANs at remote areas. There are several ways to establish WANs using different types of technologies, devices, and connections.

The Physical Layer and the Data Link Layer of OSI Reference Model work together to provide data across several types of network. Protocols and standards of LAN define how network devices are fairly close together, hence the name. On the other hand, the protocols and standards of WAN define how to network devices that are quite apart. Both types of networks implement the same functions of Physical Layer and Data Link Later, but they follow separate mechanisms.

The primary distinction between LANs and WANs includes the distance between the devices, but still able to share information. LANs are often used within a building or even nearby buildings by using optical cables that are appropriate for Ethernet. WAN connections usually run much longer distances compared to Ethernet LANs – across cities and even between states and continents.

Aside from LANs and WANs, the term Metropolitan Area Network (MAN) is also used for networks that extend between buildings. This is often used for connections that does not extend as far as a WAN, but generally covers a metropolitan area.

Physical Layer Point to Point WAN

The Physical Layer defines the particulars of data from one device to another through a medium. Regardless of the type of data transmitted, the sender will be required to actually transmit the bits to the device in form of waveforms or physical signals.

Point-to-Point WANs connects two sites, by allowing a service provider to set up a circuit. The service provider will provide the circuit and will also install devices at both ends of the circuit. This type of WAN connection is also known as a leased line because it is always available and you can use it any time you want so long as you pay for it.

High Level Data Link Protocol

High Level Data Link Protocol or HDLC is a basic data link protocol, which performs several basic functions on Point to Point serial links. The basic HDLC frame does not have a protocol field to determine the type of packet within the HDLC frame. The HDLC trailer contains a Frame Check Sequence (FCS), which allows the destination router to check if the frame has errors while moving and eliminate the frame if necessary.

HDLC Configuration

By default, HDLC is being used in Cisco IOS Software as Data Link Protocol on serial interfaces. To create an efficient point-to-point leased line connection between two routers, you must order a leased line first. When the leased line has already been provisioned, you can complete the needed cables between the routers at the two ends. Then, you can configure the IP addresses and use a no shutdown command if the interface is on administrative shutdown.

Point-to-Point Protocol (PPP)

Similar to HDLC, Point-to-Point Protocol is also used in serial links. But PPP is added with more advanced features compared with HDLC. This protocol is flexible and can provide support for both asynchronous and synchronous links. The type of protocol contained in the header allows several Layer 3 protocols to be transported over the same PPP link. It also supports authentication and two main mechanisms: Challenge Handshake Authentication Protocol

(CHAP) and Password Authentication Protocol (PAP). PPP has control measures for every higher-layer protocol supported by PPP, which allows easier integration and support.

The configuration of the PPP is rather direct without the authentication configuration. Take note that the authentication for PPP is not mandatory, and a link can still be established even without authentication. As a matter of fact, the only change here in comparison with HDLC configuration is that you need to use the command: encapsulation ppp while you are in the configuration mode.

How to Troubleshoot Serial Links

Ideally, you need to configure a point-to-point link for PPP or HDLC and all will run smoothly. But in your career as a network associate or administrator, you will often find yourself in a setting when the link fails to work properly.

A basic ping command can help you find out if the configured serial link with PPP or HDLC is capable of forwarding IP packets. If you can easily ping the IP address on the router's serial interface on the other end of the link, it is sufficient proof that the link is working. Otherwise, you need to resolve the issue. The problem could be related to the functions of the

OSI Layers 1, 2, and 3. The best approach to isolate the problem is to use the command: **show ip interface** and analyze the protocol and line status.

Conclusion

Thank you again for purchasing this book!

I hope this book was able to help you to understand the basic concepts of computer networking and the intricacies of Cisco Routing & Switching.

The next step is to try setting up your home lab with your own Cisco routers and switches, so you can practice what you are learning.

Finally, if you enjoyed this book, then I'd like to ask you for a favor, would you be kind enough to leave a review for this book on Amazon? It'd be greatly appreciated!

Thank you and good luck!

Preview of 'Python Programming For Beginners'

If you enjoyed JavaScript For Beginners you're sure to love this book!

Chapter 1: Introduction to Python

If you typically work with computers, you will eventually find that there are certain tasks that you want to automate. For instance, you want to perform a search and replace over a huge amount of text files. You may also want to rearrange and rename a group of picture files in a complex manner. Perhaps, you would want to create a specialized graphical user interface (GUI) application, a computer game, or a custom database.

If you are a professional software developer, you may need to work with Java, C, or C++ libraries. However, you may find that the usual cycle for writing, compiling, testing, and re-compiling is too slow. Maybe you are creating a test suite for a library and think that writing the test code is tedious. Perhaps, you have created a program that can use an extension language and you do not want to implement and design an entire new language for the application.

If any of these cases apply to you, then Python is the perfect programming language for you. You can write Windows batch files or a UNIX shell script for your tasks. Just take note that shell scripts are most ideal for changing text data and moving around files. They are not ideal for games or GUI applications.

Python is easy to use and available on UNIX, Windows, and Mac OS X operating systems. It will allow you to quickly finish your tasks. It is a real programming language that offers much more support and structure for large programs than batch files and shell scripts. In addition, it offers much more error checking than C language.

Python is a high level language; therefore, it has built in high level data types, such as dictionaries and flexible arrays. It is also applicable to a bigger problem domain than Perl or Awk due to its general data types.

Through Python, you can split programs into modules for the purpose of reusing in other programs. It includes a vast collection of standard modules that you can use as reference. Some of these modules offer system calls, file I/O, sockets, and interfaces for GUI toolkits such as Tk.

Moreover, Python is an interpreted language that can save you so much time when you develop programs because linking and compilation are no longer necessary. You can use the interpreter interactively, making it easier to experiment with the features of the programming language. You will also find it easier to test functions and write throw-away programs. Python is also an efficient desk calculator.

Furthermore, Python allows programs to be written readably and compactly. Most of the programs created in Python are much shorter than Java, C, or C++. This is due to the following reasons:

- Statement grouping is performed by indentation rather than using brackets in the beginning and the end.
- The high level data types let you express complex operations in one statement.
- There are no argument or variable declarations required.

Python is actually extensible. So if you are knowledgeable in C language, it would be easy for you to add new modules or built-in functions to the interpreter. You would also be able to link programs to libraries, perform critical operations at high speeds, and link the interpreter to an application created in C and utilize it as a command language or extension for that particular application.

Python was developed by Guido van Rossum in the 1980's. Just like Perl, its source code is available under the GNU General Public License (GPL). It is case sensitive, which means that uppercase and lowercase characters require caution to be used. For instance, the words 'Harlequin', 'HARLEQUIN', and 'Harlequin' are all considered different terms.

And no, Python was not named after a reptile. It was, in fact, named after a television show called Monty Python's Flying Circus. References to the Monty Python skits in documentations are allowed and actually encouraged. How fun is that?

Chapter 2: Learn The Basics

The syntax of Python is simple and straightforward. The language actually encourages programmers to create programs without the use of prepared or boilerplate code. The print directive is the simplest directive. It prints out a line and includes a newline.

Python has two major versions: Python 2 and Python 3. These two versions are different from each other. Python 2 is more common and more supported than Python 3, but the latter supports newer features and is more semantically correct.

The print statement is one notable difference between the two versions. In Python 2, it is not considered as a function, allowing it to be invoked without parentheses. In Python 3, however, it is considered as a function. Hence, it should be involved with parentheses.

Interactive Mode Programming

Programs in Python can be executed in different modes of programming. When you invoke the interpreter without passing the script file as a parameter, you will obtain the following prompt:

```
$ python
Python 2.4.3 ( #1, Nov 11 2010, 13:34:43 )
[GCC 4.1.2 20080704 ( Red Hat 4.1.2 – 48 )] on linux2
Type "help", "copyright", "credits" or "license" for more information.
>>>
```

Once you see this prompt, you can type in the following text and press Enter:

```
>>> print "Hello Python World!";
```

If you are using a newer version, you have to use the print statement with parentheses:

```
>>> print ("Hello Python World!")
```

You will get the following output:

```
Hello Python World!
```

Script Mode Programming

Using a script parameter to invoke the interpreter starts the execution and goes on until the script is done. Once the script is done, the interpreter no longer becomes active.

Take a look at the following sample program. It is written in a script and has the extension *.py*.

```
print "Hello Python World!";
```

If you type in the above source code in a test.py file and run it as

```
$ python test. py
```

you will get the following output:

```
Hello Python World!
```

Another way to execute scripts is to modify the *.py* file, such as:

```
#! /usr /bin /python
print "Hello Python World!";
```

If you run it as

```
$ chmod + x test.py
$ ./test.py
```

you get the following output:

```
Hello Python World!
```

Identifiers

Identifiers are names used to identify variables, functions, classes, modules, and other objects. They start with an uppercase or lowercase letter. They may also start with an underscore (_), followed by more letters or zero, as well as digits or underscores.

In Python, you cannot use punctuation characters, such as %, @, and $ within identifiers. Since it is case sensitive, you also have to be careful with your use of identifiers. Remember that *Example* and *example* are considered as two different identifiers because they are not exactly alike.

The following are the naming conventions for identifiers:

- The class names begin with uppercase letters. All other identifiers begin with lowercase letters.
- If an identifier ends with two trailing underscores, it is a language-defined special name.
- Identifiers that have only one leading underscore indicate that they are private.
- Identifiers that have two leading underscores indicate that they are strongly private.

Reserved Words

The reserved words in Python are words that cannot be used as variables, constants, or any other identifier names. These keywords can only have lowercase letters. The following are the reserved words in Python:

And	del	for	is	raise
Assert	elif	from	lambda	return
Break	else	global	Not	try
Class	except	if	or	while
Continue	exec	import	pass	with
def	finally	in	print	yield

Indentation

Indentation is a way to group statements. It is used for blocks in place of curly braces. The spaces and tabs are supported. However, standard indentation requires standard Python code to have four spaces. Consider the example as follows:

```
x = 1
if x == 1 :
    # indented four spaces
    print "x is 1."
```

Variables and Types

As you have learned, Python is object oriented. It is not statically typed. Hence, there is no need for you to declare variables before you declare their type or use them. Each variable is an object.

Numbers

Two types of numbers are supported in Python, and these are floating point numbers and integers. Complex numbers are also supported, though. Anyway, in order for you to define an integer, you have to use this syntax:

    myint = 5

If you want to define a floating point number, can either use this notation:

    myfloat = 5.0

or this one:

    myfloat = float (5)

Pick up your copy of '<u>Python Programing For Beginners</u>' and continue your journey with the powerful and easy to learn Python programming.